MY
LIFE
IN
TAP

SAVION!

BY
SAVION
GLOVER
AND
BRUCE
WEBER

WILLIAM MORROW AND COMPANY, NEW YORK

Published by William Morrow and Company, Inc.
1350 Avenue of the Americas, New York, N.Y. 10019
www.williammorrow.com

Printed in the United States of America.
Book and jacket design by Paula Kelly

10 9 8 7 6 5 4 3 2 1

Library of Congress Cataloging-in-Publication Data
Glover, Savion.
Savion! my life in tap by Savion Glover and Bruce Weber.
p.   cm.
Summary: Examines the life and career of the young
tap dancer who speaks with his feet and who choreographed the
Tony Award–winning Broadway show "Bring in 'da Noise, Bring in 'da Funk."
ISBN 0-688-15629-0
1. Glover, Savion—Juvenile literature.   2. Dancers—United States—Biography—
Juvenile literature.   3. Choreographers—United States—Biography—Juvenile literature.
4. Tap dancing—United States—History—Juvenile literature.   [1. Glover, Savion.
2. Dancers.   3. Choreographers.   4. Afro-Americans—Biography.]
I. Weber, Bruce.   II. Title.   III. Title: My life in tap.   GV1785.G56A3 2000
792.7'8—dc21   [b]   99-31547   CIP AC

CONTENTS

Gregory Hines
congratulates
Savion for
receiving the 1996
Tony Award for
Best Choreography
for his work on
*Bring in 'da Noise,
Bring in 'da Funk.*

FOREWORD

BY GREGORY HINES

I REMEMBER THE FIRST TIME I SAW SAVION GLOVER DANCE. **Paris, fall of 1985. Sitting down in the theater for the Friday evening performance of** *Black and Blue,* **I felt a mixture of excitement and concern. It was not enough for me that great living legends like Jimmy Slyde, Bunny Briggs, Lon Chaney, Ralph Brown, Dianne Walker, Buster Brown, and George Hillman had all raved to me about Savion's tap skills and stage presence. No, I had to see for myself if this twelve-year-old tap dancer was indeed something special.**

You see, over the years I often heard about some "young phenom" everyone was heralding as the next Teddy Hale/Baby Lawrence (improvisational tap masters), only to be disappointed after seeing them. I would usually find a very cute and adorable young person with mostly basic tap skills. When the moment came that night in Paris for Savion to take the stage, I'm sure I was sitting forward in my seat.

As he moved out onto the stage, right away I could see...how cute and adorable he was. Uh-oh, I thought, here we go again. Then he began to dance, and as I watched him, I'm sure I must have leaned even further forward in my seat. All the things I had heard about this young boy were true. All the praise became gospel. It was all there—the speed, the clarity, the vocabulary, the power (even then he hit the floor hard), and the ease. His tapping would have been impressive for a dancer of any age, but he was only twelve years old— relaxed and confident onstage, with just that hint of cockiness all the great tap dancers enjoy. My mouth hung open in amazement as he nailed step after step. Yes, he was a great tap dancer at twelve, doing Jimmy's slides, Ralph's

heel work, Lon's syncopations, and throwing Buster's rhythms all around the stage. Now I began to understand why Henry LeTang had called him the Sponge.

Sitting in the audience watching *Savion Glover Downtown* at New York's Variety Theater, now almost fifteen years later, I feel much the same way I did that night in Paris. Except now I know what to expect. Or do I? As I sit watching Savion dance now, of course I see some of the great steps I've seen him do before. But then he goes completely off on a tangent filled with new and fantastic steps I've never seen from him or anyone else. I can tell, by his own reaction to what he's doing, that it's all new to him too. He's all the way out. Out in a zone reserved for folks like Miles Davis, John Coltrane, Ella Fitzgerald, and Duke Ellington. A

HE'S ALL THE WAY OUT WHERE THE AIR IS SO...

no man's land where risk is fun and the air is so fine and rare that few breathe it. It's the air of genius. Yes, I'm saying it: GENIUS. I've felt it for a long time now, but never said it within Savion's earshot, for fear of putting undue pressure on him to live up to any expectations I might have for him. Now I feel fine with it. Because he's up to it. He's all the way up to it. In my humble estimation, he's the greatest tap dancer to ever lace up a pair of Capezios or any other tap shoes. Yes, that's my story and I'm stickin' to it.

Savion Glover has redefined tap dancing. And it can never be the same again. Tap dancing must move forward. Forward from what Savion has established. It can't go back. I also feel that tap dancers don't really reach their prime dancing years until around their midforties. Savion is now in his twenties. Can you imagine the incredible steps and choreography to come from Mr. Glover when he reaches his prime? The beautiful images he will paint with his heart and feet? I can't!

In addition to Savion's being the great artist he is, he is also a good man. I am even more proud of his development as a fine citizen of this world than I am of his great tap skills. Now, Savion's amazing mother, Yvette, would most certainly give "all praise to Jesus Christ" for Savion's completeness. And I respect that in her. But me? Well, I know she'll get upset with me, but I'm gonna split the credit fifty-fifty between Yvette and Jesus. I'm just in awe of what she has done in raising three fine sons—Carlton, Abron, and Savion—by herself. *Alone.* I watched her make sure Savion stayed focused and at the same time make sure tap dancing remained fun for him. When Savion wanted to play basketball (he can dunk, by the way) rather than practice tap, Yvette would say, "Go ahead, baby, go play some ball." Yvette made sure Savion had a childhood—a "stage life" *and* a "real life"—and that he was able to grow in a well-rounded way. To see the love Yvette has given her boys has been a real privilege for me.

Tap dancing is all about possibilities.

There are no limits to what a person can do with tap shoes on. Whenever I give a master class, I always begin by dancing for the students. I try to do steps to impress them. To amaze them. All the while I encourage them to try to steal my steps.* I try to show them some of what's there for them to express if they work for it. Dream it and reach for it. Push for it. Yes, and even steal some of it.

For me, sitting in an audience watching Savion Glover tap dance is to be reminded of all those beautiful, fantastic, powerful possibilities. And if Savion knows I'm in the audience, he'll do a step he's stolen from me. Just for me to see. It thrills me and he knows it. Of course he'll do it at MACH 3 WARP SPEED...but hey, I can dream, can't I? ■

STEALING STEPS is as much a part of the fabric of tap dancing as tap lessons are. The incomparable John Bubbles once told me how, "back in the day," he liked to purposely shake up tap dancers. He would go sit in the front row of a vaudeville theater for a show. When the tap dancer came onstage, Bubbles would take out a pad and pencil and pretend to write down the steps. Sometimes this caused the dancer onstage to speed up his or her tempos, to try to thwart the attempted thievery. Bubbles always got a good laugh out of that particular game. He was an ornery guy, but he would have adored Savion Glover. Maybe even as much as I do!

FINE AND RARE THAT FEW BREATHE IT

UH-DUH-**BAP!**

In a small dance studio on Manhattan's West Side, an argument rages.

Fuh-duh-duhh-**BAP!**

"Naw, naw!"

The argument is wordless, but it isn't soundless. This is a dance troupe, Not Your Ordinary Tappers, arguing with their feet—conversation among shoes rattling on a wooden floor.

Fuh-**BAP!**

"Wha'?"

One of the newer dancers has been having trouble with the wing step, in which a dancer leaps off the floor, kicks one foot to one side, and executes several hits on the floor with the other. A couple of the others are showing him how it's done.

Then Savion Glover, the leader of the group, steps in. "Dig it! Dig it!" he says, and then goes on with his feet:

Fuh-duh-**BAP**-duh-duh!

After an emphatic left heel stroke he manages two extra hits on the floor with other parts of the shoe before the right foot—the wing foot—flying off to the side comes to earth.

A silence in the room. There. That's settled.

Just in his twenties, Savion Glover is the settler of all arguments about tap dancing, the resolver of all questions, even the big one: Who's the best?

"Savvy's just put a whole other energy into it, leaving everybody in the dust," says tap legend Jimmy Slyde, who is more than seventy years old and still smooth. "But that's what it's all about."

Savion is the artistic grandson of some of tap's most revered figures, people like Jimmy Slyde, Honi Coles, Chuck Green, Lon Chaney, and Bunny Briggs, and heir to the generation of dancers led by the Hines brothers, Gregory and Maurice. As a child, then as a teenager, he took his place beside them in such Broadway productions as *The Tap Dance Kid, Black and Blue,* and *Jelly's Last Jam* and in the film *Tap.*

But coming to adulthood in the 1990s, Savion grew up with sounds that his elders never heard, and the music from his shoes reflects this; his feet speak hip-hop. Watching Savion dance, *listening* to him dance, one hears the rhythms of a boom box rap or a funky blues. *Bring in 'da Noise, Bring in 'da Funk,* the Tony Award–winning Broadway show he choreographed, brought the history of rhythm in America up-to-date and in the process made tap dancing cool again. Savion is the first young tapper in a generation to have imitators, and almost all by himself he has reawakened an art form.

It's a little hard to imagine such accomplishment in one so young. But in manner and appearance, he's still youthful—sweet-tempered, prone to goofiness, and with strangers as polite as a boy in church.

He's a baby face with a beard, a pucker-mouthed boy-man, dressed ordinarily in baggy unmatched clothing, shoes perennially untied, with tight spirals of hair sprouting on his head like young coral. Gangly, lithe, and athletic, he has bunched muscles in his calves and long, beveled ankles that make it seem as if his feet are dangling loosely off the end of them like castanets. Those feet are a remarkable physical thing—size 12½ EE—big for a dancer but, more important, with an array of seemingly independent parts.

"Drummers play drums, dancers play the floor," he's fond of saying. Watch him. Watch him for just a few seconds, and you count a dozen or more places on his feet that hit the floor and make different sounds: a whole rattletrap full of thwacks, clacks, tippy-tippies, thunks, sweeps, swishes, and slams. Plus, he's loud. Savion likes loud. Gregory Hines says Savion hits the floor harder than anyone he's ever seen, and he claims Savion can be heard tapping on carpet.

"The Pied Tapper," Hines calls him, the Michael Jordan of tap—though perhaps a better comparison would be to Larry Bird

Savion performs at the State Theater in New Brunswick, New Jersey.

and Magic Johnson, the basketball stars of the 1980s who propelled their game to the vast popularity it enjoys today. Indeed, in the wake of Savion's early success and early fame, there are signs that tapping is now more popular in this country than it has ever been before. Tap festivals now take place throughout the United States; the International Tap Association, a group founded in 1988 to keep tappers informed of tap activities, has doubled in size since 1993; and the success here of such shows as Ireland's *Riverdance* testifies to a surge in appreciation of the noise and funk that dancers everywhere can bring with their feet.

By now you've probably seen Savion dancing with his mirrored reflection in an advertisement for Coca-Cola. Or with the rap star/producer Puff Daddy in a music video on MTV. Or on his own ABC special. Or with the country rock singer Hank Williams, Jr., in the opening credits for *ABC's Monday Night Football.* Or acting in a TV special on Showtime. Or performing with Not Your Ordinary Tappers (NYOTs) onstage in their touring show. You might see his choreography in a new musical about the Harlem Globetrotters. Throw in his performance on *Sesame Street,* and you've got a young artist engaging a remarkably wide cross section of the American mainstream.

Tap, to flourish in the twenty-first century, needs his stardom. But it also needs his dancing. In the past those two things have not been easily reconciled, but if anyone can do it, Savion is the man.

He is unique in this regard, a young artist with the future of an art form at his feet. ●

PEOPLE ALWAYS WANT TO KNOW WHERE AN IDEA FOR A STEP COMES FROM, where an idea for a dance comes from. It's hard to know. I don't think about process too much. I think about hittin', which is what tappers do. We hit! It's a gut thing, an artist's thing. You *know* when you're hittin'. When you're straight layin' it down, communicating, saying something, expressing yourself, getting on the floor the rhythm you live by, that's hittin'. Hittin' can be so many things. All you have to do is look at the different dancers, the

Savion sets the pace for members of his dance troupe NYOTs
(Not Your Ordinary Tappers)—Jason Samuels, Ayodele Casel,
Omar Edwards, and Abron Glover.

way they hit, the way they have all different styles. If another dancer says to you, "Yo, you hit!" that's what it's about.

Not too long ago this lady came up to me, and she said, "Yo, man, I saw your show, and you rocked!" Now, nobody ever said that to me before, but I dug it. That, to me, meant she saw me and I got her, I put it *down*! I *hit*! People, not dancers, they usually say, "I saw your performance; you were really good," and I'm always, like, Thanks a lot. But she was like, Hey, man, you rocked! And I was thrilled. I was, like, *Yo!* Like, she *said* that to me. That, to me, is hittin'.

I'm just always hearing things, hearing rhythms. It's always been that way. And it's not like I sit down and practice hearing things, or walk through a room and say, "Now I'm going to come up with some complicated stuff." It just happens, onstage it happens. Something's in my head, and I want to get it out.

Sometimes, not always, I wake up with rhythms in my head, like I've been dreaming about them, and I start making them right away with my mouth. Diggi-diddi diggi-diddi. Nothing complicated. Rudiments. It's my brain warming up for the day, the morning exercises.

I think in rhythms, and I talk that way too. It's weird, but I can say to you, "tickety BLOO kah tickety bloo kah SHUCK," and I'll know exactly what I'm talking about, and another dancer will too. I can have a whole conversation that way. It's what we do when we dance, anyway, when we "cypha," picking up on something

TICKETY

BLO

TICKETY

KaH

SHU

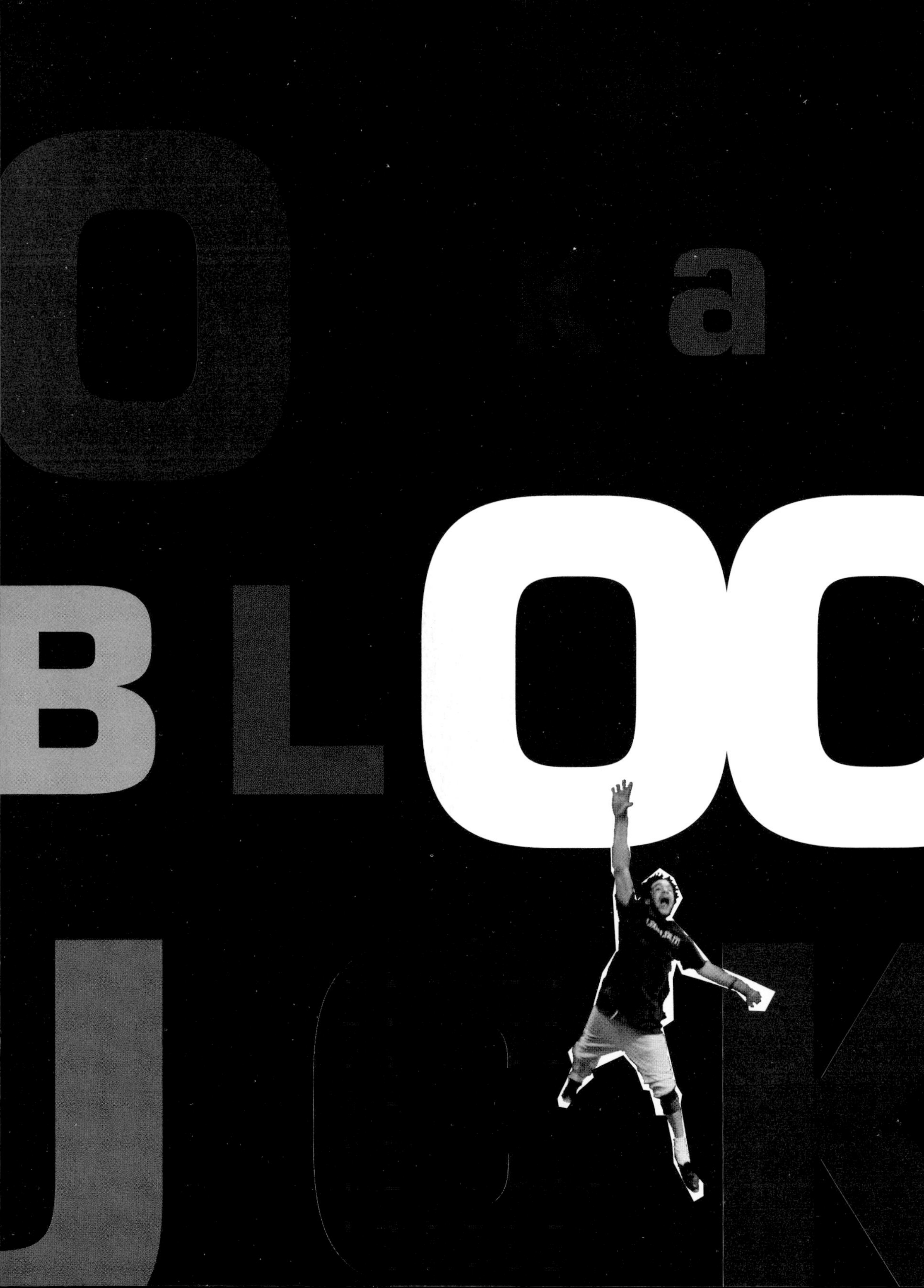
O a
BLOO
J K

somebody else is doing and flipping it, passing it along, challenging the next guy to pick up on what I'm doing.

Does an idea come to me through my ears first or through my feet first? I don't know. You have some dancers who can produce through the feet but can't sing what they're doing. It's good to be able to do both. Sometimes I'll hear it, then I'll do it. Sometimes I'll do it, then I'll hear it.

Sometimes I'll hear something on the street, in the subway, or maybe I'll hear a lick in some music I'm listening to that'll stick with me. Like, the other day I was thinking about a step I'd done in a PBS special with Tommy Tune and Gregory Hines, and suddenly I heard the step different, the same exact step. DUM di DUM didi DUM didi eeliyoudumDUM dadum DUMdaDUM deedle ee deedle eedle DUM.

That was the original, but all of a sudden I heard it starting in a different place. It didn't start on one, you know, the downbeat of a measure; it started on three. So now I'm thinking about it, and I can't get it out of my head. I don't know what sparked it, but I've been flipping it in my head all week, and I haven't had the chance to do it in my shoes yet. I have to get it out

of my head now, *do* the step, to match what I'm hearing with my feet. I can sit around going eedle eedle eedle all day long, but the thing is: Can I really *do* that? Make those sounds? What does my body look like? Not that I care what I look like so much, but can I get to the next sound from where I am? Is there a turn there? Are my feet in the air? Am I fighting gravity? That's the hard part, actually producing the step through the feet.

I know my feet, all about them. It's like my feet are the drums, and my shoes are the sticks. So if I'm hearing a bass sound in my head, where is that bass? Well, I have different tones. My left heel is stronger, for some reason, than my right; it's my bass drum. My right heel is like the floor tom-tom. I can get a snare out of my right toe, a whip sound, not putting it down on the floor hard, but kind of whipping the floor with it. I get the sounds of a top tom-tom from the balls of my feet. The hi-hat is a sneaky one. I do it with a slight toe lift, either foot, so like a drummer, I can slip it in there anytime. And if I want cymbals, crash crash, that's landing flat, both feet, full strength on the floor, full weight on both feet. That's the cymbals.

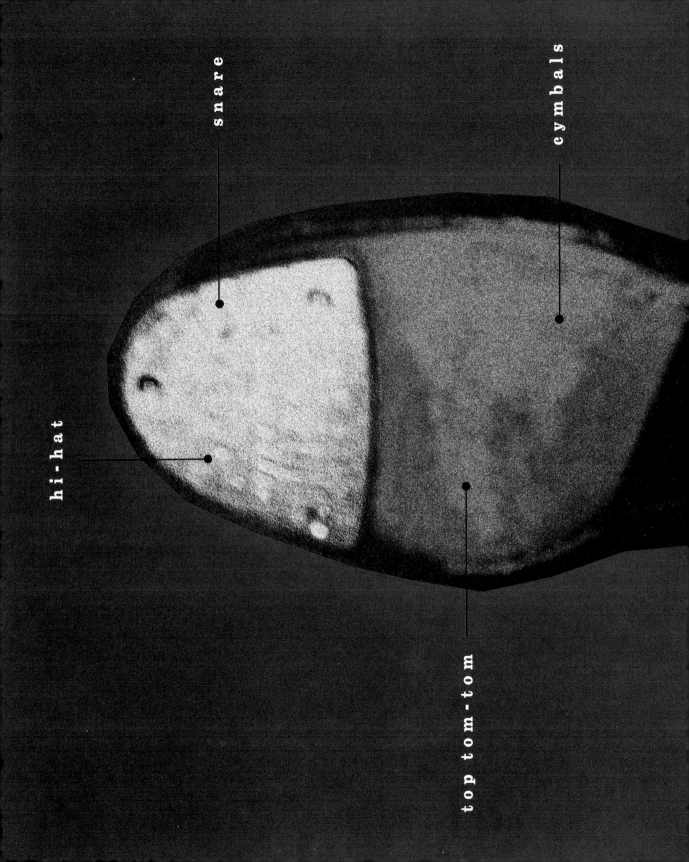

snare

cymbals

hi-hat

top tom-tom

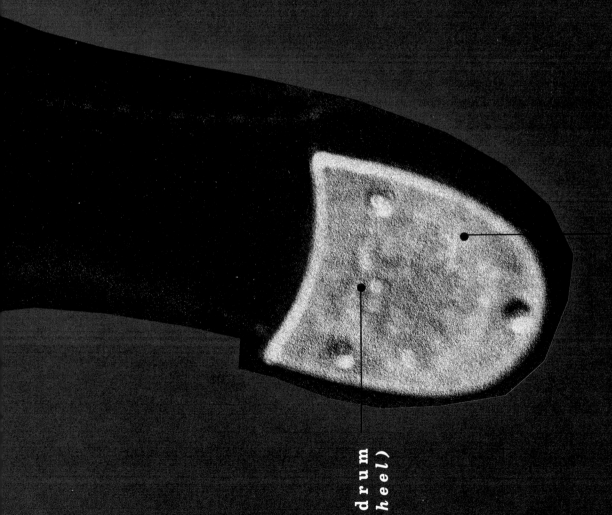

bass drum
(*left heel*)

floor tom-tom (*right heel*)

21

Tap, to thrive in the next century, needs Savion's stardom. Here he takes a break on the set of his ABC special *Savion Glover's Nu York.*

So I've got a whole drum set down there. And knowing where all those sounds are, knowing where I'm trying to get them from, that's how I go about creating the step.

I don't worry about the look of it so much. Choreography comes later, when I'm putting together a whole piece. I'm into the sound; for me, when I'm hittin', layin' it down, it's all about the sound.

But really I'm an improv artist most of all, and I don't even know what I've done once the moment is gone. A lot of times I look at footage of myself and I'm like, Whoa! What was that? Rewind it.

Rewind it. I have to stay with the step, right there, hold it in my head while it's fresh and make an effort to keep it there, or I'll forget about it, it's gone.

But tapping isn't about repertoire anyway, knowing steps, memorizing steps. I mean, you got to know how to do things, the rudiments, but it's about making sounds, bringing sounds, bringing the funk.

People ask me, "Aren't you afraid you're going to run out of rhythms, run out of sounds?" Naw, naw. No way. They're everywhere, all the time. That's why I have so much dancing to do. ■

"I don't even know what I've done once the moment is gone. A lot of times I look at footage of myself & I'm like, Whoa! What was that? REWIND IT, REWIND IT."

Charles ("Honi") Coles in the 1970s. He later became one of several tappers who most inspired Savion in his early dance years.

LiSTENIN'

MOST TAPPERS AND TAP HISTORIANS WILL TELL YOU that until recently tap has been in decline for a good long time. Its heyday was the 1920s and 1930s, before the movies and television introduced a new kind of mass entertainment and before rock and roll arrived and changed popular dancing. Tap never went away, but it did step aside.

Savion is starting to change that by finding a way both to honor the past and to forge new ground. As a boy imitating the master dancers of an older generation, he learned not just to dance but to hold the dance in high regard, to revere its history, its community, its etiquette, its respect-your-elders tradition.

It was in the early 1990s, during the time Savion was in *Jelly's Last Jam* on Broadway, that he began to find his own "voice," so to speak. He had grown up listening to rap music and the hip-hop sounds then emerging in youth culture, and it occurred to him, Why am I not dancing to the music I *listen* to?

"With all this Broadway stuff, what people don't get about Savion is that he's a hip-hop artist," said Reg E. Gaines, the poet who wrote the book for *Bring in 'da Noise, Bring in 'da Funk*. "That's the story about Savion. His thing is hip-hop."

In other words, just as Savion's art is of the past, it is also of the moment.

Tap is an American art form, but like most things American, it's full of elements that arrived here from elsewhere. It's also mostly an African-American form, but like jazz, its history would be incomplete without acknowledging the contributions of white artists. Most historians say that tap began to evolve when West African musical culture, based on drumming and rhythm, was brought to this hemisphere with the slaves. It spread through the Caribbean, mixed with the syncopations of the islands, and then came to this country. Immigrants from Ireland and France and England and Holland had already settled here with their own traditions. What resulted was a cross-fertilization of European and African cultures. As people shared with each other—and borrowed and stole—new kinds of songs emerged. New beats. New rhythms. New dances.

Dance and music have always been partners, and right around the turn of the century a new kind of music arose that was to change the course of both art forms in this country. That was the soulful lamentation known as the blues, which was born in the Mississippi cotton fields from a mixture of African work chants and Christian hymns. The blues gave the world a new sound. And as the country became more industrialized and as travel became more common, the blues traveled north from New Orleans to Kansas City and Chicago, picking up regional influences along the way and giving birth to ragtime, swing, and jazz.

Tap evolved along with the music, pushed ahead by innovators in dance clubs like the famous Hoofers Club in Harlem, a basement room at One Hundred Thirty-first Street and Seventh Avenue. During the 1920s and 1930s, it was the favorite gathering spot of dancers, what the jazz historians Marshall and Jean Stearns called "the acknowledged headquarters of American dance—tap variety." The tradition of tap challenges (or cutting sessions) was established there. One at a time dancers would try to outdo one another, and it became an unofficial law that copying someone else's steps—exactly—was a crime. And innovation was the result.

There King Rastus Brown, the greatest performer of buck dancing—a flat-footed combination of shuffles and taps— overlapped with Bill ("Bojangles") Robinson. Robinson, with his gift for comedy and his engaging public image, was the first celebrity tapper, but he was also an

innovator: He lifted tap from the flat to the balls of the feet, bringing tap up on its toes. There too a dancer named John Bubbles demonstrated his off-the-beat accents, snapping his toes to the floor or dropping his heels hard, adding new rhythms to the tap repertoire.

In the 1940s bebop jazz changed the world's ears with its frenzied, complex rhythms. Baby Lawrence, another innovative tapper who was also a singer for the Art Tatum band, brought the high-energy drive of the era's music to the dance. "Every time I heard Art Tatum play the piano, I had a crazy impulse to move my feet as fast as he moved his fingers," Lawrence told the Stearnses for their famous book *Jazz Dance*, which was published in 1968.

The list of great tap dancers does not end there, of course, but many of the names are nowadays obscure: Charles ("Honi") Coles, who was a friend and mentor to Gregory Hines; Pegleg Bates, who could match anyone, step for step, in spite of a wooden leg; the Condos brothers, Steve, Frank, and Nick, who added the wing step to the tap repertoire; Bunny Briggs, Leonard Reed, Ralph Brown, Jimmy Slyde, Chuck Green, Lon Chaney, and dozens of others. That they are largely unknown has nothing to do with their skill, but rather to do with how times changed.

There were many reasons for the decline of tap during the decades that followed. For one thing, jazz drumming overtook tap as the main force for innovation in musical rhythm. For another, most Americans began to experience tap through the movies and television, which made the dance just a part of something new and huge, the entertainment business. The best-known dancers of the forties and fifties, Fred Astaire and Gene Kelly, were celebrities whose fame as singers and movie stars superseded their fame as dancers. Then, when Elvis Presley and rock and roll came along, the focus of popular dancing became not the feet but the body.

In the 1960s, an era of social ferment and youthful rebellion, tap more or less vanished from view, perceived as a relic

Learning from tap elders gave Savion a strong base from which his own style grew. In the Broadway show *Black and Blue*, he danced alongside such greats as Ralph Brown, Ted Levy, Jimmy Slyde, Bunny Briggs, Lon Chaney, and Bernard Manners (front).

Using the peg of his wooden leg to create a strong rhythm, Pegleg Bates
dazzled audiences with his showmanship in the 1930s, '40s, and '50s.

from an outdated America. Young African-Americans in particular turned away from the form; they felt it to be reminiscent of a time when racial stereotyping was acceptable in popular culture. The image of a smiling tap dancer, shuffling on a stage for the appreciation of white audiences, was unacceptable. Unlike earlier periods, when developments in tap followed changes in music, in the sixties tap did not accompany the sounds arising out of the African-American community. People didn't tap to rock and roll. People didn't tap to soul music or Motown.

"Unfortunately a lot of us did feel that way," said Sandra Burton, a dance historian and professor of dance at Williams College in Massachusetts. "African Americans have been wounded by those stereotypes inherited from minstrel shows. We didn't want to see ourselves strutting and gliding. The artists were hurt because they seemed to represent something we couldn't be proud of. But the thing about tap is that it's a genuine, vernacular art form. It's now linked to hip-hop just as it used to be linked to bebop. So I see it as moving now into its next phase."

That's largely thanks to Savion. ●

WE DIDN'T WANT TO SEE OURSELVES STRUTTIN' & GLIDIN'

I'M YOUNG TO BE PREACHING ABOUT HISTORY, BUT I KNOW I COULDN'T DO WHAT I do if it wasn't for all the cats who came before me, who developed the steps and the spirit and the culture of tap. And I was lucky, of course, because when I was just a kid, I got to hang out with some of the best. And they encouraged me to pick up where they left off.

For instance, I think about Honi Coles sometimes. He died a couple of years ago, but he was smooth, man. He loved for me to do *his* steps and then take it into a back flip and a split. We'd be somewhere, at a tap festival or someplace, and I'd finish a performance, do what I thought was a big finish, and then he'd call me back out. This was when I was maybe twelve, thirteen and he'd already had a couple of strokes. I'd get out there again, and he'd say, "Okay, keep the crowd going, do *my* thing." He meant a rudimentary step, an exercise made up by Henry LeTang, a dancer and a great teacher: shiggi diggi diggi diggi right right right, shiggi diggi diggi diggi left left left.

And he'd want me to do that and then bounce into the split, and the crowd would go crazy. It was just acrobatics, nothing that I invented, but I remember

In *Bring in 'da Noise, Bring in 'da Funk,* Savion acts as puppeteer for a L'il Darlin' doll during "The Uncle Huck-a-Buck Song," a number that responds to the stereotype of the African-American tap dancer.

feeling that his spirit was passing through
me to the audience, that I was helping
pass that along.

Honi and Buster Brown and Lon
Chaney and Jimmy Slyde and Ralph Brown
and Chuck Green—they taught me the
rules. And you have to know the rules,
because that's respecting the tradition.
Take the hoofer's line, for instance. That's
where everybody's doing a paddle and roll
and one dancer at a time takes a solo turn.
There are rules, but the rules are
unspoken, almost secret. The main thing
is you got to finish the phrase of the
man before you, finish it and then add

something of your own. And if you don't,
you'll be cut by the next man,
embarrassed, you'll have your own step
flipped back on you. You can spit on
someone through the dance. You can
murder someone through the dance.
Dancers do that all the time. It's part
of our ritual to be competitive. And you
know when you've been cut. It's terrible,
especially if a lot of people recognize
it. If it's like that, you'll get everybody
going: "Ooooooooooo . . ."

But if I'm in there with Slyde, I'm
thinking first, I respect him as a man, and
second, I respect him as a dancer, so I'm

BOTTOM: Savion jams to the hip-hop beat of Wyclef Jean during a Brooklyn street fair filmed for *Savion Glover's Nu York.*

not going to go out there and attempt to cut Jimmy Slyde. Every now and then some young cat will do a step that Slyde has been doing forever or maybe a step that Slyde taught him. Every time that happens, Slyde tells him right back through the dance: Thank you very much, but you missed something. That's cuttin'. That's the rules. That's respecting our history.

I spent a long time learning, staying in the background. It wasn't until just a few years ago that I really started doing my own thing. Up until that time, when I'd be working out with some other dancers, I'd just be scatting—dancers do that, improvising just the way jazz singers do— and laying down steps that were familiar to the old hoofers. I would go up to St. Nick's, which is a place on One Hundred Fiftieth Street, where the old cats hang out, and I'd dance with them, and they'd know what I was about, spitting scats, doing something really jazzy.

But then I'd go to places downtown, hip-hop clubs like PS 50, where people were my age, and if I tried to do what I did uptown, no one would understand that there. There was an emcee at PS 50, a DJ called KRS 1, his real name was Kris Parker, and I would just try to spit out

what he was saying, the feel of it. It was just a simple rhythm, the milk beat we call it: BOOM BOOM BOOM bahbuhBOOM BOOM. But I started dancing it, bringing that beat, and people started saying, "Yo, this cat is bringing it to us."

I listen to all kinds of music—jazz, classical, rock, rhythm and blues, gospel, calypso. My mom played it all in the house when we were growing up. And then among my brothers and me it was hip-hop and reggae. But it didn't occur to me to dance to what I was listening to. And the thing was, it didn't occur to the dancers of the generation before me. You know, in the late sixties and the seventies, funk was in. But when it came time to tap-dance, dancers didn't dance to the music they were partying to. That played a big part in what happened to tap, why it got so restricted. The dancers themselves didn't keep their act current with the culture. That's what I'm trying to do. I dance to jazz and old stuff and whatever, but mostly it's going to be hip-hop, something with a funky bass line.

I still hear criticism sometimes, cats saying, "Oh, now Savion's doing hip-hop dance." As if it's some kind of special dance. But that's not how I see it. In fact,

let's get it straight. It's not hip-hop tap. It's not rap tap. It's hoofing.

It's
tap
dancing.

Savion's mother noted his talent for music and rhythm from his earliest years.

D R U M M i N '

YOU MIGHT SAY THAT SAVION was born to dance, but his mother thinks it started before that. Savion, she says, was tapping in the womb.

"I was working for a judge, as an assistant, when I was pregnant with Savion," Yvette Glover says. "And when I would type, and the carriage would automatically return, he'd walk, he'd follow it, in my stomach. You could see him move."

When Savion was born, on November 19, 1973, life was not exactly easy for Yvette and her family. Yvette raised Savion and his two older brothers, Carlton and Abron, in Newark, New Jersey, a once-bustling city that was on the down slide after the race riots of the late 1960s. They lived first in a house that they shared with Yvette's mom and brother, occasionally a few cousins, and also the owners of the house. In 1979 Yvette and the boys moved to their own house in a city development, but they ended up sharing that too, with Yvette's mother and two close friends of the family. Yvette never had her own bedroom until 1992, when Savion bought her a house on a leafy suburban street in New Jersey—just a few miles away from hardscrabble Newark, but a world apart.

Yvette raised her three sons, who have three different fathers, with a combination of devotion, determination, and religious faith, and the four of them remain intensely close. The boys, grown men now, still call their mother Mommy, and they have a word for their togetherness: *fam-fam.* But even to a mother devoted to all her children, Savion was marked, early on, as special.

"I knew from the womb that he was going to be something, because God told me," Yvette says. "He gave me the name. I'm not a fanatic, but I am religious, and when I was in the hospital, I said, 'God, I don't have a name for this baby.' And I closed my eyes, and the slate of a blackboard, as black as it can be, appeared before me, and He wrote the name out in script—He didn't print it; it was in script: *Savior.* And I said, 'Now, You know I can't name him Savior.' So I took out the *r* and put in the *n.*"

It's always a bit of a mystery where surpassing talent comes from, but music and dancing were certainly in Savion's genes. Yvette's mother, Anna Lundy Lewis, was a church organist of local renown, and her father, Wilbert Lewis, was a singer and keyboardist who played the Borscht Belt hotels in the Catskills.

Yvette herself is a gospel and jazz singer.

Savion's father, Willie Mitchell, was a carpenter by trade, but he could dance. "That's what drew me to him," Yvette says. "His rhythm. The whole movement of his physique. The man could dance. He can dance to this day."

Clues to Savion's gift began to emerge when he was astonishingly young. Before he was a year old, he was responding when his grandmother sang to him—by singing back. Before he could stand up, he was drumming.

"When he was crawling, he was maybe nine, ten months old, he'd go under my sink and take out the pots and whatever would make a sound, and he would start banging," Yvette says. "This was before he walked. He'd just have to be making sounds. He would beat up on the wall, he'd beat on anything. He'd beat on me or you if you were there."

And when he learned to walk, it was not with his feet flat on the ground. Rather Savion raised himself onto his curled toes, parading around the house almost on pointe.

"I remember I thought something crazy was going on," says Abron, who was three years old when his little brother rose up from a crawl. "He got up

HE'D GO UNDER MY SINK AND TAKE OUT THE POTS AND...

and walked on the knuckles of his toes. And not even walking. He was jumping up and down on them. Boing! Boing! Boing!"

Such inklings of a gift called for encouragement, and when Savion was four and a half, his mother enrolled him in suzuki classes at the Newark School for Performing Arts.

"He didn't have any drums at home, and that's why I had to get him out of there," Yvette says, laughing. "He was destroying my house."

Savion quickly placed out of the suzuki classes and into the regular classes with older children, and he was given a scholarship. This was where he received his first real musical instruction, and he began to play the drums.

By the time he was six, he was ready for the world to hear him. Indeed, if Savion's meteoric rise can be traced back to the moment of launching, it was on a winter afternoon in early 1980. Yvette had brought Savion along to her gospel group rehearsal at the home of her manager, Rudy Stevenson. At one point the group took a break, and from somewhere else in the house a set of drums could be heard. It was Savion,

whaling away. Stevenson went to check on him and never came back to finish the rehearsal.

That was the day Savion's performing career began. Stevenson had three young sons of his own, all of them musicians. One played bass; one played saxophone and trumpet and flute; and the youngest, who was Savion's age, played piano. Stevenson put his sons together with Savion into a group they called Three Plus, and it was not long before they were playing in parks, at street fairs, even occasionally at weddings and parties.

In the spring of 1982, Stevenson got Three Plus a gig playing at the Broadway Dance Center, a well-regarded dance school, and it was that day that Yvette Glover inadvertently set about changing dance history.

"I remember I was sitting there, and during intermission, it was either after or before the boys played, Frank Hatchett announced they were taking enrollment for dance school," Yvette recalls. "And I said to myself, Now look, if Savion's got this much rhythm, then sign him up for dance. And that's what I did!" ●

STARTED PLAYING DRUMS IN SUZUKI CLASS when I could first walk, I don't know, when I was three or four or something like this. I'd go in there and start banging on some drum or on the piano or the xylophone, and they eventually moved me up a level into the regular drum class, I think because I was just banging too much noise. I just couldn't stop banging around.

Meanwhile at home I used to play everything, just everything, my mother tells me. I do remember putting on shows for her. This was when I was maybe three years old. She would come home from work, and I'd have the knives and forks out from the drawers and the pots and the pans set up like drums. I figured out you could get different tones out of the big pots and the little pots and the teakettle and the colander. And Carlton would play the guitar, and Abron would be dancing or something like that, and we'd have a show for her, all the boys. We even did this after we got into elementary school. After school we'd come home and be practicing all day.

I stopped taking drum lessons when I got into the band. Three Plus. I was the plus. Me and Rudy Stevenson's kids. We were good, man. We did standards like "Take the A Train," "In a Sentimental

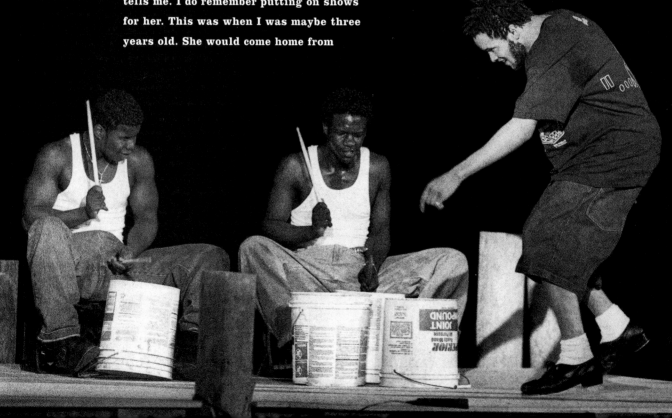

Mood," but we could also kick it. We'd have the people rockin', man. We played schools, outside festivals. We'd just set up on the street and do performances. Basically we would perform anywhere.

So at some point, I don't remember how it happened exactly, but we were playing for some benefit at the Broadway Dance Center. I remember that's where I first saw Lon Chaney and Chuck Green.

I was maybe seven years old, and all up to this time I had never thought of dancing. It never crossed my mind, even though I was hip to it. I was hip to Fred Astaire–type dancing, his kind of smooth dancing, and I dug it, but I'd never seen rhythm dancing before. It wasn't until that day that I'd ever seen Chaney and Chuck do their thing. And I watched them and I was like, Wow! They had different rhythms going than I had ever heard before. And it was with their feet! They were just really laying down all the rhythms. And I was totally fascinated.

And I remember I followed Chaney into the dressing room, this big bear kind of a man with a low, rumbly voice, and he told me he had been a drummer before he was a dancer. And he was like, "You were doing some good rhythms on the drums," and I was just a little kid, so I didn't say anything. And he said, "You should try to dance." The funny thing is I didn't say anything to my mom. She just signed me up. Me and my brothers. The next thing I knew we were in class.

I can't say I was actually prepared. I had some boots, three-quarter-length cowboy boots I went to tap school in, beige boots. But they had a hard bottom, and that's how I got the sound. After a while, when we got tap shoes, then it was, like, Wow, this is what it's about. And I started thinking about speed, being fast. As a matter of fact, I used to think it was all about being fast. Diggitydiggitydiggitydiggity again and again, always about speed, diggitydiggitydiggitydiggity. My brothers were the same way, but I'll tell you this, once I started, I was different from my brothers, because I would always dance. Always. ■

Hoofing to the beat of the street in *Dancing under the Stars* at the Delacorte Theater in Central Park. With the accompaniment of Drummin' Too Deep (Larry Wright and J.R. Crawford), Savion illustrates how his connection to complex rhythm is rooted in drumming.

I would dance
walking. I wo
I was waiting
I would dance
dance in th s
dance. I was ju

when I was
uld dance when
for the bus.
on the bed,
hower. I'd just
st happy to be...

HOOFIN'

O NCE SAVION WAS ENROLLED AT THE BROADWAY DANCE CENTER, he began to feed his hunger for dance. It wasn't long before he began performing in tap festivals with icons of the form—Lon Chaney, Jimmy Slyde, Chuck Green, Honi Coles, Buster Brown, Ralph Brown, Bunny Briggs, Henry LeTang, and George Hillman—who would begin to teach him the history of hittin'. And soon he began not just the dance lessons but the life lessons that would make him the torchbearer for a very proud tradition.

It was at the Broadway Dance Center that show business came calling for Savion. There, in 1983, the producers of a Broadway musical, *The Tap Dance Kid*, had created a workshop for young tappers to build a ready pool of talent for the show. In mid-1984, before he turned eleven, Savion auditioned for the workshop.

"We were, all of us, struck dumb," said Norman Rothstein, the show's general manager, recalling the reaction of the show's producers, the casting agent, and the choreographers. "Though he was not the strongest singer in the school or the strongest actor, we knew we were in the presence of, if not genius, then something akin to it. We just knew it."

The Tap Dance Kid had opened on Broadway the previous December, bringing renewed attention to tapping with its exuberant choreography and its story of a boy living on Roosevelt Island in New York's East River who pursues his dream to dance. The show won two Tony Awards and ran almost eight hundred performances, long enough that its young star, Alfonso Ribeiro, and his replacement, Jimmy Tate, completed their runs in the show and went on to other things. Savion ended up as the third Tap Dance Kid; after several months of honing his dance technique and amplifying his vocabulary of steps in the workshop, he took over the title part in September 1984.

As Willie, the son of a New York lawyer who believes that tap dancing is a belittling thing for African-Americans, Savion captured the spirit of a boy born to dance. Rattling his taps on the floor of his stage bedroom, on the sidewalks of the city, even on the tram between his middle-class home on Roosevelt Island and the showbiz world of Manhattan, he danced the dreams of youth, literally following in the steps of Willie's heroes—Fred Astaire, Gene Kelly, and Bill ("Bojangles") Robinson. He went on to play in some three hundred performances, until the show closed on August 11, 1985.

This was the beginning of a life change for Savion. For one thing, he changed schools—from Queen of Angels, a Catholic school in Newark, to the Professional Children's School in Manhattan. After a year, he moved on to the East Harlem Performing Arts School, where he felt more comfortable. (At the age of eighteen he graduated from Arts High School, back in Newark.)

It was also the beginning of Savion's professional apprenticeship, a period when he danced alongside established tappers, became used to performing in front of audiences, and learned the rudiments of working a stage. As a dancer he aped his elders, mastering the conventional steps—the shuffle, the paddle and roll, the buck and wing—and fusing them to a youthful enthusiasm and athletic, muscular grace. It would be years before he would begin to develop his own style, but as a dancer he was, if not yet original, fast and inexhaustible.

In 1988 Savion went to Paris to perform in *Black and Blue,* a revue featuring the blues singers Ruth Brown, Sondra Reeves Phillips, Carrie Smith, and Linda Hopkins, as well as three generations of tappers. Savion performed in the traditional hoofers' line, taking a solo turn along with Bunny Briggs, Jimmy Slyde, Lon Chaney, Ralph Brown, and George Hillman, with whom he danced a spiffy duet. Later, in the Broadway run of the show, this number changed altogether, evolving into a much-praised trio with Savion and two young girls—Cyd Glover (no relation) and Dormeshia Sumbry—dancing up and down a three-step staircase. His performances in the Broadway run earned him a Tony Award nomination, making him

An early head shot of a budding Broadway star

one of the youngest-ever Tony nominees.

Black and Blue was a remarkable opportunity for a young man not only to advance his skills but also to see the world. By his own admission, though, Savion didn't see as much of Paris as he did the inside of the dressing rooms of the old-timers he was coming to idolize.

"Savion was always asking questions, and watching, watching, watching," said Dianne Walker, a tapper in the show who became so close to Savion that he began calling her Aunt Dianne. "If Slyde and Chaney were playing cards, Savion would watch them play cards. He just couldn't get enough of those guys."

Jimmy Slyde laughed, remembering that Savion always seemed to be underfoot, pestering everyone with his questions. "We started calling him the sponge," he said.

It was also in Paris, before *Black and Blue* moved across the ocean to Broadway, that Savion first got to know Gregory Hines, the beginning of a mentor-protégé relationship that continues to this day. Hines came to see the show, and afterward he recruited Savion for a part in the movie *Tap*. A number of the great old dancers were in it too, and so was Sammy Davis, Jr.

They would film it together the next year.

In the movie Savion plays the part he was more or less playing in real life: a young boy and a would-be tap dancer who looks up to his elders and in particular to Hines's character. Hines plays a dancer who turned to crime and went to prison and who now attempts to stay on the straight and narrow after getting out of jail. In many ways the story is also about the redemptive power of dance.

Savion has a dance scene all to himself in the film, and it shows off everything he had learned to that point from Hines and the others. His on-screen presence was charming, and his star quality increasingly difficult not to see. Soon afterward the producers of *Sesame Street* invited him to appear on the famous children's show as a character named Savion, perhaps the first recognition outside the dance world that Savion was destined to be a leader with his very own audience.

By 1991 he was a regular on the show, a friendly neighborhood presence, familiarizing the likes of Elmo and Big Bird with the joys of tap. It was a role Savion played intermittently for five years, while thousands, maybe millions, of kids grew up to the sounds of his feet. For the first

"Savion would watch them play cards. He just couldn't get enough of those guys." Savion always seemed to be underfoot, pestering everyone with his questions. "We started calling him the sponge."

time, perhaps, tapping became a part of cultural education in America.

That brought Savion to the pivotal show in his young career: *Jelly's Last Jam,* the musical stage biography of the arrogant and charismatic jazz pianist Jelly Roll Morton. By then he was eighteen years old, and for the first time onstage he looked more like a man than a boy. And for the first time his gifts as a dancer and an actor were an integral part of a show and its very conception. Unlike in *Tap Dance Kid,* where he was a replacement, or *Black and Blue,* where he was part of an ensemble, in *Jelly's Last Jam,* Savion played Jelly Roll as a youth; the relationship between him and Hines, as the adult Jelly Roll, was a critical one.

The show itself was marvelously inventive, and it contained a number that marked Savion as a star on the horizon. Nearly halfway through Act II, Jelly and Young Jelly, Hines and Savion, performed a duet that represented the casting off of Jelly Roll's innocent youth. As part of the number the two dancers engaged in a challenge, one doing a step and the other matching it and improving on it.

As the show's run went on, the challenges became more intense, often going on longer than the producers or any of the other performers expected and often pushing Hines to the far edge of his repertoire. Anyone who saw the show could tell what was going on: The torch of tap was being passed, one generation to the next.

"He can tap-dance faster and harder and cleaner than anyone I've ever seen or heard of," Hines said. "He hits the floor harder than anybody, and to do it, he lifts his foot up the least. It doesn't make any sense. There must be some explanation, but you tell me what it is. What's the explanation for Michael Jordan? Except that's a disservice to Savion because at twenty, Michael Jordan was not the basketball player that Savion was a tap dancer."

Hines, whom Savion has come to think of as a father figure, can talk a long time about Savion's virtues. "When I was his age, I looked up to Honi Coles, Sandman Sims, Sammy Davis," Hines said. "I'm twenty-eight years older than Savion, and he's been looking up to me. Now we've got teenage kids and they're looking up to him. Savion's the one who will lead tap into the next century." ●

The stairway dance in *Black and Blue* (performed in the United States with Dormeshia Sumbry and Cyd Glover), in addition to his other performances in the show, earned Savion a Tony Award nomination.

For young Savion, dancing in *Black and Blue* was an important growth experience.

I LOOK BACK ON IT NOW, AND IT SEEMS LIKE EVERYTHING happened so fast. It's hard to believe all that has happened since I was twelve years old and getting ready to go onstage for the first time in *Tap Dance Kid.* I mean, just a few years ago, in *Tap,* I was hangin' with Sammy Davis, Jr., and he was on the set drinking Kool-Aid and wearing a do-rag. It was red Kool-Aid, I remember, and he drank it in a big mug. Like regular folks. Sammy Davis, man!

And then I was on *Sesame Street,* which was also cool, a nice vibe. That's when people started recognizing me on the street. Kids. And I noticed a lot of them were wearing their hats askew, like I did on the show. I liked Elmo; he was my favorite, so innocent even when he was doing wrong stuff.

Anyway, looking back to *Tap Dance Kid,* I can see I knew nothing, nothing. I went through all the rehearsals, all the understudy's rehearsals, and what did I know about scripts and scenes and blocking and upstaging and cues and exit lines and all that? I had no idea how to change clothes between scenes in time to get back on. Someone's going to change

me? Whoa! Hinton Battle, the star, he was always on us kids about warming up, getting ready. And other stuff too, like hygiene. I can remember him pulling me aside and saying, "Yo, man, I don't know if you're using any deodorant, but you better get some." And he was right. I *was* funky that day.

My opening night I was nervous, out of my mind nervous. Butterflies in my stomach and everywhere else. I'm not that great a singer to begin with, but that night my voice was shaky as milk. The only thing that saved me was my family. There was a scene in the show on the Roosevelt Island tram, and I rode across the stage on this tram, and while I was riding it, I saw my mom for the first time, and this relaxing feeling came over me. I saw her face, and it was, like, relief. I was comfortable from then on.

What I learned from *The Tap Dance Kid* was the basics, really the basics. The basic basics. Familiarity with the stage. How to position myself. How to prepare. How to listen. How to react to the audience. I took it on myself to learn the theater, walked around it as if I were working there, went up on the catwalks to see what the guys do up there, backstage, all that. It was, like, I'm here to perform, but I'm also interested in what's behind the secret door. I guess I was ready for it to be real, not so magical anymore. You know, I was part of it. The magician has to know what the explanation for his magic is.

Anyway, that was why *Tap Dance Kid* was important for me. As for my performance, I didn't really feel like I was performing. That was *my* life up there, and being onstage was just like sitting around the kitchen table telling a story about what happened to me that day. And every night, when we'd take our solo bow, I felt like: These people aren't clapping for me, for Savion; they're clapping for Willie, the Tap Dance Kid. I never felt like Savion was taking that bow.

It was after I got started on *Black and Blue* that I began to understand it didn't have to be that way. During the show I'd go out and do double times, big steps, trying to please the audience, and then afterward I was hanging out with Slyde and Chaney, and just by watching them, I saw it wasn't about pleasing the audience; it was about expressing yourself. It didn't happen right away. You don't just wake up and find your voice, your style. It has to develop. But during *Black and Blue* was when I started realizing I could create my own kind of dance. Up to that point all I was doing was dancing.

It wasn't anything they told me, not really. It was just being there every day.

During rehearsals in New York I'd just be looking—at Slyde, at Chaney, at Chuck, even at the women, like Dianne—and I'd be watching them, saying to myself: This is nothing like what I was taught in dance class. The sounds, their bodies, the way they handled themselves. Once we got over to Paris, I'm in the wings watching them, I'm in Chaney's back pocket when he comes offstage. I was like that with all of them. I just wanted to follow them around. I don't know why; they were interesting, is all. This was a club I wanted to join.

I was learning how to hang out, to enjoy. People think I hung out with them and only learned dance. But remember, I had no father image in my life. And these cats were men, and they were accepting me, and I was just this little kid running around, and they let me hang out with them everywhere. We went out. We went to clubs. You ask what they taught me? Everything. About life. About being a man. About how to be. The point is I still spend time conversating with myself about these men. It doesn't matter where I am, something one of them said'll hit me, mad things, like footnotes—"Make sure you put the right foot first, even if it's the left one," or "If you can't flow with it, don't go with it"—and I'll have to ask myself: Are you talking about the dance or life?

Slyde would drop info on me. He's such a wise man. Through the dance he'd tell

FAR LEFT: Though Savion starred in the movie *Tap* with idols like Gregory Hines and Sammy Davis, Jr., in this scene from the movie he has a few admirers of his own.

me, "Swing a little, sing the song." I would always come out and do double time, all the time fast, fast, and Slyde told me, "You should try swinging." And the first time I tried it, I danced for seven minutes, and my breathing was different. I was relaxed, not tense, not holding my breath. I felt like I was singing what I was dancing. So that was something he told me that helped my dancing. But he was always telling me, "Stay comfortable." Now is that about just dancing?

And Chaney would tell me, "Hit it! Put it *down,* young man!" and I understand that as a dancer and as a man. I can take that information about the dance and use it in my everyday life. It translates. You see what I'm saying? And I remember Chuck telling me, "Keep on the cardboard." What does that mean? I have no idea. "Keep on the cardboard." But I remember it, and I know, like twenty years from now, it'll come to me: Damn! That's what Chuck meant!

When we came back to Broadway, I was really trying to find myself as a tap dancer. My performance began to change, and even my mom noticed. I wasn't smiling as much, not trying to *please* so much. It wasn't, like, Hey, I'm here, it's show time! anymore. It was more, like, Hey, let's go out and dance! Forget what *they* think they want to see. Chaney, Slyde, those cats—they saw my progress. It was real. I was finally asking, Why am I performing?

And then came *Jelly's,* which was really the turning point, the first time I ever performed in a show and felt like it was me, Savion, up there, getting the applause and not the character I was pretending to be. But mostly *Jelly's* was important to me because of Gregory. He took me under his wing after *Tap,* and it

Savion at center stage with the cast of *The Tap Dance Kid*

was Gregory who made sure I got cast in *Jelly's*.

He wasn't like Slyde, who's more a grandfather type, with all the mysterious wisdom he lays on you. For me, knowing Gregory is like knowing you have a pops but not meeting him until you're twenty years old, and it turns out he's been very cool all this time. We met in Paris when he came to see *Black and Blue*, and little did I know he was setting up this audition for *Tap*. Right away he was calling me Save, which only my brothers call me. After that we just started hanging out. We'd go to Knicks games; he'd come over to family barbecues.

Anyway, that relationship made it easy for me to, like, complete my education as a tap dancer, putting the finishing touches on all the stuff that Slyde and them had begun to teach me. And in *Jelly's,* I was playing the kid and he was playing the adult, and it seemed perfect to me that we were just there being two sides of the same person. And that number in the second act, Jelly's Isolation Dance, that was the highlight. I would do everything he did, right away, right away, keep spitting back to him what he was handing me, and we'd really be laying it down some nights. It was supposed to be a five-minute number, but it went on longer and longer and longer, we'd go on and on, jamming, and some nights people would just gather in the wings and watch. It was six, seven, eight minutes of joy every performance. And yeah, it felt like he was passing the torch down to me every night.

It was humbling. Still is. ■

Savion in rehearsal for *Bring in 'da Noise,
Bring in 'da Funk,* which would push him further out
into the mainstream and the forefront of tap

BRINGIN' 'DA NOISE

AFTER SAVION HAD COMPLETED
his run on Broadway and on the national tour of *Jelly's Last Jam,* he was ready for his
own artistic showcase—the chance to speak in his own voice, with the language of
tap. So in the summer of 1995, Savion selected several African-American artists—
including young dancers like Baakari Wilder and Jimmy Hill, the singer Ann Duquesnay,
and the poet Reg E. Gaines—to come together with *Jelly's Last Jam* director
George Wolfe to talk about rhythm and history and a new show.

"Why don't we tell the history of racism through Savion's feet?" Gaines
recalls asking the group.

The show turned out to be *Bring in 'da Noise, Bring in 'da Funk,* which opened at
the Joseph Papp Public Theater—where Wolfe was now producer for the New York
Shakespeare Festival—on November 15, 1995, and then moved to Broadway's
Ambassador Theater the following spring. It was the show that made Savion a star,
and that won him a Tony Award for his choreography. In many ways, it changed the
stodgy world of Broadway theater forever, opening it up to hip-hop culture for the
first time. It brought the dance and theater art of young, contemporary African-
Americans to an older, largely white, mainstream audience.

Perhaps the most powerful sign that something new was (pardon the
expression) afoot was that many of the artists gathered in the rehearsal room at the

I want to tell a story, give people some history

New York Public Theater also found Savion's vision unfamiliar and elusive.

"I just want to bring the noise, bring the funk," he said, as an explanation of the show he envisioned. But *noise* and *funk* are not just words to Savion; they are concepts, they are an attitude. What they mean to him is more easily expressed in rhythm than in language.

"We all sat down at a round table," Gaines recalled. "There were maybe twenty people, and there was a tape recorder going, and George asked, 'What does "bring the noise and bring the funk" mean?' And the older people there were all saying, 'Oh, the funky chicken, and James Brown.' And then Savion said, 'Nah, nah. Y'all don't get it. Say me and Dulé, we want to go out dancing one night. We're gonna be, like, "Yo, bro, we gonna go out and *dance* tonight, and we gonna bring the *noise!*"'

"And I took the tape home and listened to it, and I thought, This could be the whole show, defining what that means. So the first thing I wrote down when I got home was: 'Bring the noise, bring the funk, bring the best you got.' What it meant was doing the best you can; the 'noise' was *excellence*."

Gaines's script—sometimes angry, sometimes lyrical, always defiant—sought to express the essence of noisiness and funkiness throughout American history, in a kind of singsongy streetwise incantation. This served as the show's narrative spine, and Savion and Wolfe—with the assistance of the dancers, the drummers, and the singers—draped a terrific spectacle upon it. The show didn't turn out exactly to be a history of racism told through Savion's feet; it was more like a *response* to racism as told through Savion's feet.

In all of the show's scenes—from the slave ships arriving on American shores to the exploitation of African-American labor in factories to the sleek sassiness of Harlem high society to contemporary hip-hop street life—shoes and bucket drums and pots and pans and garbage can lids tapped out a vibrant accompaniment. The story was in one sense the history of America and in another sense the evolution of American rhythm, using the concept of "'da beat" as a stirring metaphor for the enduring black spirit. The subtitle for the show said a lot: *A Tap/Rap Discourse on the Staying Power of the Beat*.

The dancing was loud, furious, exuberant, syncopated, new; it bore the stamp of the rap music, the hip-hop sound that young African-Americans had made their anthem. Never before had a tap dancer heard the kind of noise and funk that Savion was hearing, at least no one who could re-create them with his feet.

Near the end of the show Savion made the connection between the historical and the personal. In a solo dance, enacted in front of a folding set of mirrors so the audience could watch him from several angles at once, he performed a number called "Green, Chaney, Buster, Slyde." The number was an eloquent statement about the place of tap, and its practitioners, in both the black American experience and his own. In it, Savion danced in the styles of his heroes, and in a voice-over narration, he spoke movingly about what they meant to him. "They helped me find myself," he repeated to the audience every night as he danced before the mirror. "I just like started like doin' Chaney, I started doin' Slyde, I started doin' all their steps and their steps started just like changing my style. I just started like hittin', reachin' for rhythms."

It was a remarkably mature moment for an artist who, at the time of the show's opening, was twenty-one years old. 'Da beat goes on, he was saying, and this is where I fit in. I'm carrying on where these great men left off.

I have a big responsibility, he was saying. And I'm up to it. Just watch me. ●

IT WAS DURING *JELLY* THAT GEORGE STARTED TALKING ABOUT HOW AFTERWARD HE WOULD LIKE TO DO some new work with me. He asked me if I had a chance to do a show, what would I do? And this was perfect timing, because I felt like after *Jelly* I'd gotten to where I'd learned how to do my thing. I felt it, that I was ready to step out on my own. I said to him right away, "I want to bring the noise. I want to bring it to the people. I want to do straight tap dance, bring it to them raw."

And he asked me who would I want to be involved, and I knew exactly, all these people whose work I'd admired or who I'd worked with. Reg Gaines, I'd just seen him once, on MTV, I think, reciting his poems, and he was like, raw, the words he was saying were real as death. And I'd kept it in my mind, like, Who is this brother? I'd never met him, but George found him and brought him down to the Public. Ann Duquesnay, we were in *Jelly's Last Jam* together. But I remember I'd heard her sing at something my mom was doing, a gospel revue at the Victory Theater. She sang this song, man, "Believe in Yourself," and that was it for me. I didn't know her back then. But I

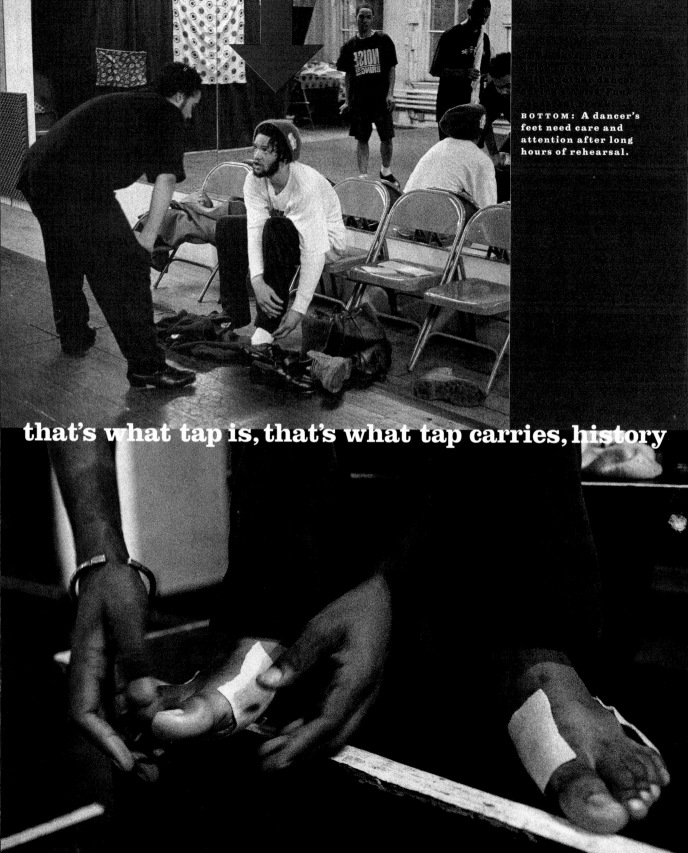

that's what tap is, that's what tap carries, history

I just want to bring the noise...

remembered her singing it from I don't know how many years ago.

The bucket drummers, J.R. Crawford and Larry Wright, I had met them when I was doing *Tap Dance Kid;* they'd be playing on the street when I came out after the show. And Jimmy Tate, you know, he was Willie before I was, and then we danced together in *Jelly's.* And some of the younger dancers, like Baakari Wilder and Vincent Bingham and Dulé Hill, all these guys are cats I knew and had been dancing with through the years. So it wasn't a show anybody had to audition for; it was, like, let's all come together and do this thing we're always talking about. Word up.

So George is asking me, "What do you mean you want to bring it?" And I'm saying, "I want to tell the world about Jimmy Slyde, about Buster, about Chuck and Chaney. And at the same time I want to tell a story, give the people some history, because that's what tap is, that's what tap carries, history, and not just the history of tap but what was going on while tap dancing was going on."

Once I got the dancers in the rehearsal room, we just started making up routines. It wasn't, like, Okay, we got to do an industrial dance that takes place in a factory. It was like, Here are our ideas, how can we make a scene out of that? We had J.R. and Larry in there, the bucket drummers, and they could just get a sound out of anything. A pot, a pan, the button on the top of your hat. So they were in rehearsal one day playing the walls, and I was just fooling around, swinging from a pipe, and my leg comes up and J.R., he starts to play the bottom of my shoe. And George was there, and he looked up, and he said, "Can you do a routine where he plays the bottom of your shoe?"

But that's how everything happened. We'd be sitting around and see Larry or J.R. beating on each other, and George would say, "What if you had pots and pans hanging on you all over your body?" And they came back with "The Pan Handlers" number. We didn't go in with a plan; we'd go in there and make things up every day. George would watch, and Reg would listen, and then he'd go off and write. And the musicians, they'd be off somewhere else, doing their thing. But it was like we were all hanging out together, and it worked.

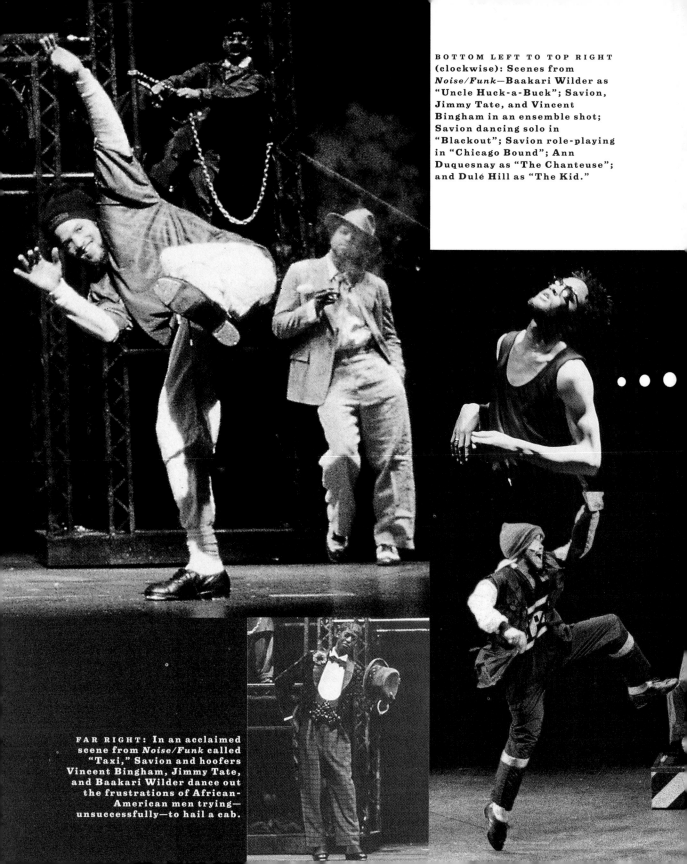

BOTTOM LEFT TO TOP RIGHT (clockwise): Scenes from *Noise/Funk*—Baakari Wilder as "Uncle Huck-a-Buck"; Savion, Jimmy Tate, and Vincent Bingham in an ensemble shot; Savion dancing solo in "Blackout"; Savion role-playing in "Chicago Bound"; Ann Duquesnay as "The Chanteuse"; and Dulé Hill as "The Kid."

FAR RIGHT: In an acclaimed scene from *Noise/Funk* called "Taxi," Savion and hoofers Vincent Bingham, Jimmy Tate, and Baakari Wilder dance out the frustrations of African-American men trying—unsuccessfully—to hail a cab.

bring the funk

In a powerful performance that takes the emotional impact of his dance to a new level, Savion evokes images of African-American slavery during "Slave Ships" (from *Noise/Funk*). Slaves were forbidden drums and musical instruments, so many of them used their feet to speak in rhythms.

I knew this from the start. *Bring in 'da Noise* would have to have in it everything I'd learned, onstage, offstage, about the dance, about the theater, about the audience. And every style of dance came out of me: soft shoe, ragtime, all of it. So what I'm saying is, this was like giving birth for me, giving birth to myself as an artist. Before *Noise/Funk*—when I was doing *Tap Dance Kid* and *Black and Blue* and *Jelly's*—that was like being pregnant, nourishing this baby with all the knowledge I had. And then I just put together all this information, and this inspiration, from all those years hanging out, with my mom and my brothers, and with Slyde and Chaney and Chuck, all these years of being in the world. And then I took this killer cast, and we just put it down. So that's what *Noise/Funk* was to me, introducing myself to the world. My first baby. Me. ■

H O L D i N '
i T D o W N

CHUCK GREEN DIED IN 1997, AND IN OCTOBER I WENT TO HIS MEMORIAL at St. Peter's in Manhattan. And I had a visit with Slyde there. We were up in the church, and everybody had left. It was just me and Slyde sitting in the church. And you have to understand, these guys were like my guardians, I feel like I'm part of this family, they're like the Gambinos or something. So here I am in this church, after this celebration of Chuck's life. And the whole thing is over, and Slyde, he's dropping the word on me; I'm always asking him for advice, so he gave me some. He said, "Right now, where we've taken tap, we got to keep it there, keep it in the public eye, keep it seen, keep it on TV, keep it onstage, keep something happening for the dance," and through that keep something happening for myself. And he had an idea for me; he said I need to go ahead and create a new cologne. Called Da Funk.

Maybe he was joking. I don't know. Is that what it takes to keep tap moving on up? Maybe it is. It's funny that getting your name out there sometimes seems more important than getting what you do out there. I mean, how many people know what hittin' is, or can recognize it when they see it, and can appreciate it when they recognize it? I'd love it if that became an expression, people saying, "We going to hit!" Like, we going to put it down, not loud, but properly.

Whatever you do, dancing or whatever, you got to hit. Don't sleep on it. Just hit. Because for me, dancing is like life. The lessons of one are the lessons of the other.

Maybe for everybody to feel that way I got to have my own cologne.

All I know is from here, I got to go and have another baby. I'm living, getting more information, more knowledge every day, and I'm turning that back into the dance. I feel like it's my duty to carry on this art form. Just from knowing cats like Slyde, knowing what they stand for, knowing they didn't get the proper recognition. I mean, I hear all the compliments, and it's lovely to me when people say I'm the best, but I'm looking at what those cats are doing, what Gregory's doing in his fifties, what Slyde's doing in his seventies, and I'm, like, Whoa, that amazes me. I know deep inside that as a tap dancer I have a lot of room to grow. And I really feel like I'm holding it down for them, for Slyde and Chaney and Chuck, and I always will be. Whether it's on Broadway or Off Broadway or in somebody's basement, somewhere somebody's going to know I'm holding it down.

Because dancing is it for me. It. Just it. There's no person, no food or drink, no movie part going to change my mind about that. I mean, in my mind I'm a tap dancer. How many people can say that? How many people can say what they are? It's one thing to say, "Okay, I'm a celebrity now, I'm going to get me a TV show." Nothing wrong with that, understand, but I'm a tap dancer first.

And if I have anything to do with it, tap is going to keep growing. It's going to have its proper place at last. I want tap to be like a baseball game, a football game, people coming to see us at Yankee Stadium. I want tap to be on TV. I want tap to be in the movies. I want tap to be massive. Worldwide. ∎

Word

u p.

ACKNOWLEDGMENTS

The publisher wishes gratefully to acknowledge Michal Daniel for his generous contribution of photographs for this book; also thanks to Carole Davis, Sarah Scheffel, Paula Kelly, Joe Guillette, Ken Howard, Mel Howard, Michael Costa, and Eric Saperstein for their assistance.

Photo credits: pages 1, 6, 10–11, 15, 22–23, 30, 34, 35, 60, 62 (top and bottom), 65 (top and bottom), 66 (and insets), 68, 69, 70, 71, 72–73: Michal Daniel; pages 3, 77: Hassan Kinley; page 4: Richard Corkery/© Daily News, L.P.; pages 9, 12: *The Star-Ledger*/New Jersey Newsphotos; pages 13, 20, 32 (top and bottom), 74, 80: © 1998 Donna Svennevik/ABC, Inc.; pages 16 (top), 42–45: courtesy of Rush Media and Coca Cola, Inc. Coca-Cola and the contour bottle are registered trademarks of The Coca-Cola Company; page 16 (bottom): © 1998 Lorenzo Bevilaqua/ABC, Inc.; pages 18–19: graphic by Paula Kelly and Joe Guillette; pages 24, 28, 31: Photographs and Prints Division/Schomberg Center for Research in Black Culture/The New York Public Library/Astor, Lenox and Tilden Foundations; pages 26–27: Ken Howard; page 36: courtesy of Yvette Glover; page 40: Michelle V. Agins/NYT Pictures, The New York Times Company; pages 46, 53, 58, 59: Martha Swope, © Time Inc.; page 49: estate of Bert Andrews; page 51: Beatriz Schiller; page 54: © 1989 Newsday, Inc. Reprinted with permission; page 56: © 1988 Tri-Star Pictures, Inc.; page 57: © 1998 Children's Television Workshop. Sesame Street Muppets © 1998 Jim Henson Company. Photograph by Richard Termine.

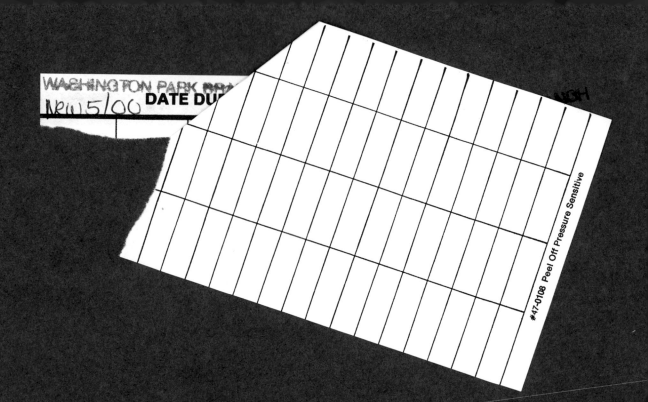

#47-0108 Peel Off Pressure Sensitive